KT-567-353

BK01414

Victoria & Albert Museum, London

# Japanische Holzschnitte

Joe Earle

Verlag Paul Haupt Bern und Stuttgart

Copyright © Joe Earle 1980
First published in 1980
by The Compton Press Ltd.
and
Pitman House Ltd.
Second impression 1982.
Published by Her Majesty's Stationery Office.

Designed by Humphrey Stone and
edited by Anthony Burton.
Photography by Ian Thomas.
Produced by Pitman Books Ltd., London.

ISBN 0 11 290387 8

Dd 696410 C40

IT IS NOT generally known that although printing is almost certainly a Chinese invention, the earliest surviving examples of printed text (with the exception of a single Korean charm) are Japanese, dating from A.D. 764, when the empress Shōtoku decreed that a million miniature pagodas should be manufactured and dedicated at leading Buddhist temples. Each pagoda was to contain a Buddhist charm on a slip of paper and the craftsmen entrusted with the task of producing these charms evidently decided to save time by printing them. There is still disagreement as to whether the charms were printed from wood or metal, but what is important for the history of the colour print is that movable type was definitely not used. In this as in all subsequent Japanese printing, except for a brief phase from about 1590 to about 1650, the impressions were taken from wood blocks carved (or perhaps, in this unique case, metal plates cast) specially for each page of text, and the experience built up over centuries of carving the intricate Japanese script formed a significant part of the technological inheritance drawn on by the men who made the blocks for the prints of the Edo period (1615–1868), with which we are chiefly concerned here.

For about three hundred years from 764 there is no evidence of printing in Japan but in 985 a complete printed copy of the huge Buddhist canon known as the *tripitaka* was brought from China by a Japanese pilgrim. This impressive publishing feat appears to have rekindled monkish interest in printing and in 1088 the first Japanese printed Buddhist text appeared. About one hundred years later we find woodblocks used for illustration for the first time in a series of decorated fan leaves in which certain repeated details were mass-produced by the use of hand-held stamps and in the same century decorative backgrounds were added to scrolls by similar means.

The popular sects of Buddhism which gained recognition during the twelfth and thirteenth centuries, with their emphasis on repeated invocations of the name of the Buddha, were a stimulus to

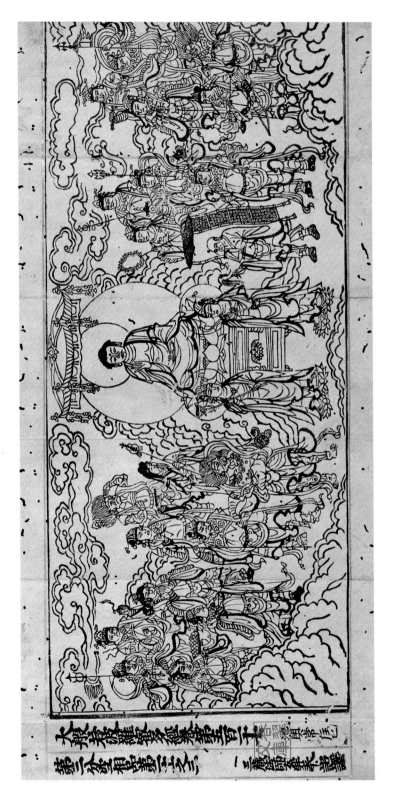

Abbildung 1

Anonym, nach einem chinesischen Original. Der Pilger Hsüan Tsang erhält den Kanon *Tripitaka* von Buddha. Titelbild zu Band 517 des *Dai Hannya-Haramitta-Kyō*, einer buddhistischen Schrift. Der Holzschnitt entstand wahrscheinlich im Kōfukuji Tempel in Nara.

Datiert 1383

26,2×47 cm

F. E. 107–1975 Geschenk Hofer

Vollendung, und einige der späteren Beispiele zeigen einen hohen Grad an Fertigkeit in bezug auf die Holzschnitt- und Druckkunst. Gleichzeitig wurde eine wachsende Anzahl buddhistischer Texte mit Titelillustrationen versehen, die sich gewöhnlich an chinesischen Vorbildern orientierten (Abb. 1); ebenso erschienen im frühen 15.Jahrhundert erstmals gedruckte Handrollen mit Illustrationen in einer eigenständig japanischen Stilrichtung.

Die bis anhin erwähnten gedruckten Werke waren alle buddhistischen Urprungs; bis etwa 1590 wurde das japanische Druckereigewerbe von Tempeln und Klöstern beherrscht. Aber von nun an war ein dramatischer Aufschwung publizistischer Aktivitäten auf dem Gebiet der illustrierten weltlichen Literatur zu verzeichnen, was ungefähr um das Jahr 1680 zum Entstehen von einzelnen gedruckten Blättern führte, zu den ersten «japanischen Holzschnitten», so wie wir heute den Begriff verwenden. Es handelt sich hier um Schwarz-Weiss-Drucke, wobei bereits in diesen frühesten Beispielen oftmals Farben, vor allem Mennige *(Tan)* und Gelb, von Hand aufgetragen wurden. Dieses Verfahren gelangte bis etwa 1715 zur Anwendung, als ein anderer roter Farbstoff pflanzlichen Ursprungs, der *Beni* genannt wurde, in Gebrauch kam. Wenig später wurde es Mode, mit Lack und Messingstaub eine luxuriösere Wirkung hervorzurufen und gewisse Bereiche eines Holzschnittes hervorzuheben. (Abb. 6 zeigt ein gut erhaltenes Beispiel.) Dann, um 1740, wurden *Beni*-Rot und Grün erstmals mittels speziell geschnittener Druckstöcke aufgetragen.

Im Gegensatz zu Einzelblättern wurde der Mehrfarbendruck bereits 1631 in Büchern verwendet, wie beispielsweise in den Diagrammen einer mathematischen Abhandlung; während des 18.Jahrhunderts wurde eine wachsende Farbpalette zur Illustration von Gedichtbänden, Handbüchern der Malerei und anderen Publikationen gedruckt. Diese frühen Leistungen waren jedoch einem ausgewählten Kreis von Kennern vorbehalten und durch chinesische Vorbilder beeinflusst. Erst um 1760 entwickelte sich der Mehrfarbendruck in einer eigenständig japanischen Stilrichtung und wurde für ein breiteres Publikum zugänglich. Ende des Jahres 1764 entschloss sich nämlich eine kleine Gruppe von Kunstliebhabern, Kalender mit mehrfarbigen Illustrationen für das neue Jahr zu bestellen, und sie beauftragten den damals wenig bekannten Künstler Suzuki Harunobu mit den Entwürfen. Die neuen Techniken ermutigten ihn, einen neuartigen Stil zu entwickeln, der aus ihm einen der grössten Namen in der Geschichte des japanischen Holzschnitts machen sollte. Bald wurden die Kalender als Einzelblätter ohne Datum neu aufgelegt, und die Zeit des volkstümlichen Mehrfarbendruckes hatte begonnen.

The traditional print was a result of the collaboration of three distinct specialists: the designer, the blockcutter and the printer. The lion's share of the credit for the finished article has always gone to the designer, by whose name the prints are known, but the contribution of the other two craftsmen was at least as great. Much of the beauty of Japanese prints lies in qualities which have in recent years become harder to appreciate now that most of us experience them through the barrier of photographic reproduction and it is just these qualities which are due to the blockcutter and the printer: the clarity and depth of the colours, the sharp precision of the details and the look and feel of the *hōsho* paper, made from the inner bark of the mulberry tree, which is soft and yet strong enough to remain stable over as many as ten printings. The efforts of these three craftsmen were coordinated by the publisher. The greatest publishers, for example Tsutaya Jūsaburō (1750–1797) could influence the whole course of the *ukiyoe* movement; Tsutaya 'discovered' or encouraged such artists as Utamaro (PLATE 11) and Sharaku and was a dominant figure during one of the great periods of the art.

The production process began with the designer, who painted a detailed line drawing on specially thin paper in a mixture of soot and glue. Occasionally this job was not done by the artist in person but entrusted to another craftsman, who set down in detail the artist's rough sketch. The completed drawing was then passed to a team of blockmakers, whose task was to interpret the designer's wishes in woodblock form. The drawing was sized to prevent wrinkling and carefully pasted face-down on to a block. The back of the paper was scraped away so that only a very thin layer was left and this remaining layer was then oiled leaving the drawing fully visible to the blockcarver. All the surface of the block was then cut away except the lines of the drawing. The job of cutting round the lines was reserved for the senior member of the carving team, who used a knife with an angled blade. Then a chisel with a rounded head was used to clear waste wood away from the areas adjacent to the cut line, thereby facilitating the more general clearing done with larger chisels. The blocks themselves were of cherrywood, cut with the grain (this yields larger blocks than end-grain cutting), seasoned for several years in clamps and then meticulously planed.

An important feature of the line block left by the first stage of cutting is the pair of marks, one at a corner and one in the middle of a side, which were used to ensure perfect registration when the colour blocks were printed. Once completed the line-block was used to produce a number of impressions (incorporating these marks) on which the designer indicated the colours he wanted for each area of the print. Colour blocks were then cut and the prints were run off.

The Japanese printing method differed considerably from the Western, above all in the fact that the paper was placed on the block (instead of the block on the paper) and rubbed on the back with a circular pad made from bamboo. It is the use of this rubbing technique, combined with the softness of the paper, which gives the colours in Japanese prints their texture and depth; often, in fact, the colours are clearly visible on the reverse. The inks used were *sumi*, the soot and glue mixture used for the original design, and a variety of vegetable and mineral pigments mixed on the block itself before each printing. Special techniques include 'blind-printing' without ink, which embosses the paper, and the wiping of colour blocks before printing so that the colour varies in intensity in the finished print.

There is an almost defiant bravura in the technical virtuosity of some of the later carvers and printers, whose intention is clearly to transcend rather than to be faithful to the woodblock medium (see, for example, PLATE 26). In the present century, however, artists of the *sōsaku hanga* (Creative Print) movement, who carry out every stage of the process themselves, have felt the need to be honest to their materials and let the process show in the finished print. It is with a work by one of these artists that the present selection concludes.

## THE BACKGROUND AND DEVELOPMENT OF THE UKIYOE STYLE

The stylistic origins of the Edo period prints are complex and to trace them in full it is necessary to go back several hundred years to the narrative scrolls in which the native pictorial style came to maturity. In these scrolls the emphasis is always on decorative effect, with strong and gorgeous colour and well-defined outlines. The early Muromachi period (fourteenth and fifteenth centuries), in which contact with Chinese civilisation was renewed after a period of isolation, saw the introduction by Zen Buddhist monks of a bold style of monochrome ink-painting, chiefly of Chinese subjects, and for some time the two schools, one native Japanese and the other of Chinese origin, remained strictly separate. In the mid-sixteenth century, as the chaotic military conditions which had prevailed for two hundred years began to improve, the numerous warlords started to commission paintings for the gloomy halls of their newly-built castles. Many of these warlords were of humble origin and were interested neither

# Der Hintergrund und die Entwicklung des Ukiyo-e-Stils

Die stilistischen Ursprünge der Holzschnitte aus der Edo-Periode sind komplex; um sie vollumfänglich aufzuzeigen, müssen wir die um einige Jahrhunderte früher entstandenen Rollbilder erzählenden Inhalts berücksichtigen, als der eigenständige japanische Malstil zu seiner Reife gelangte. In diesen Rollen mit den kräftigen und leuchtenden Farben und den bestimmten Konturen liegt die Betonung immer auf der dekorativen Wirkung. Als in der frühen Muromachi-Periode (14. und 15. Jahrhundert), nach einer Periode der Isolierung, der Kontakt mit der chinesischen Kultur erneuert worden war, führten Zen-Mönche einen kühnen Stil monochromer Tuschmalerei ein, wobei sie vor allem chinesische Themen darstellten; so führten für einige Zeit die beiden Schulen, die eine japanischen und die andere chinesischen Ursprungs, ein streng getrenntes Dasein. Als sich um die Mitte des 16. Jahrhunderts die chaotische militärische Lage zu verbessern begann, die während zweihundert Jahren geherrscht hatte, schickten sich die zahlreichen militärischen Machthaber an, Malereien für die düsteren Säle ihrer neu errichteten Schlösser in Auftrag zu geben. Viele dieser Militärbefehlshaber waren von bescheidener Herkunft und waren weder an der vorzüglichen Miniaturmalerei interessiert, die ein dahinschwindendes höfisches Leben schilderte, noch an der nüchternen Pinselmalerei der Zen-Mönche. Als Reaktion auf ihre Nachfrage entstand ein neuer prächtiger Stil, der die zeichnerische Kühnheit des chinesischen Pinselstils mit der herrlichen Farbgebung der japanischen Tradition verband. Die Paare sechsteiliger Stellwände sowie die Schiebetüren, die auf diese neue Art geschmückt wurden, gehören zu den krönenden Glanzpunkten der Momoyama-Periode (1568–1615), ja der gesamten japanischen Malkunst überhaupt.

Zunächst waren die Motive dieser Stellwände auf chinesische Weise, Szenen der klassischen Legenden sowie auf symbolische Vögel und Blumen beschränkt, aber allmählich begannen die Maler ihre Aufmerksamkeit dem täglichen Leben der damaligen Zeit zuzuwenden. Sie stellten Gesellschaften beim Betrachten der Ahornbäume dar, Feierlichkeiten in berühmten Heiligtümern, das Leben in und um die Hauptstadt Kyoto oder die fremden portugiesischen Missionare und holländischen Händler, die damals für kurze Zeit in die japanische Geschichte eindrangen. Eine wichtige zeitgenössische Anregung für die Entwicklung einer neuen Genremalerei ging von den Nara-Bildern *(Nara-e)* aus, den populären Abkömmlingen der Rollbilder erzählender Tradition, von denen viele von einer lebhaften Teilnahme an den Angelegenheiten des gewöhnlichen Volkes zeugten. Sie zeigen einen anderen Weg auf, wie die alten Malstile an neuen Themenbereichen angewandt und für ein breiteres Publikum zugänglich gemacht werden konnten.

Abbildung 2

Hishikawa Moronobu (etwa 1618–1694)
Der Dämon vom Rashōmon besucht, als Kinderfrau verkleidet, Watanabe no
Tsuna.
Etwa 1680–1690
25,1×34,6 cm
E. 1346–1922 Vermächtnis Lee

and in time both the new milieu and the paintings were referred to by a special term, *ukiyo*. This was originally a Buddhist expression meaning 'this sad world', but by about 1660 the character for the *uki* part of the word had been changed to give the meaning 'floating world', with connotations of rapidly changing fads and fashions, optimism and a general lack of thought for the morrow. Add *e*, meaning pictures, and you have *ukiyoe*, 'pictures of the floating world', the term normally used for pictorial art in this style by the Japanese themselves. The first artist (or at any rate the first artist known to us by name) to adopt this floating-world painting and combine it with the classical narrative style to produce an entirely new type of book-illustration was Hishikawa Moronobu (PLATE 2); and around 1680, as mentioned above, these illustrations began to appear in independent form.

Moronobu's talent for composition is clearly evident in the print reproduced here; another feature of his style which is not so well represented is the striking exploitation of the contrast between mass and line, for example between the solid black mass of a girl's hair and the bounding lines and complicated arabesques of her costume. It is Moronobu's use of the limitations imposed by the stark choice of black or white which has gained him the admiration of many collectors, sometimes at the expense of the multicoloured prints of the later period.

The print shows the well-known story of Watanabe nò Tsuna, who cut off a demon's arm in a fight. Disguised as Watanabe's old nurse, the demon tricked the hero into producing the arm. It then seized its severed limb and flew off screaming into the air. The subject matter allows rather close adherence to traditional narrative methods: strong diagonals and roofs left off buildings to show indoor action.

It is as well to mention, before discussing the subsequent development of *ukiyoe*, that this book, which deals only with independent prints, gives a very one sided impression. A vital contribution continued to be made by both illustrated books and paintings and many of the artists discussed below were distinguished in both these additional fields. Another type of print which is inadequately treated here is the *shunga*, erotica, although these too constitute a large part of the oeuvre of many of the most famous artists (PLATE 10). The reader should also be reminded that a number of print-designers, of whom the most prominent is perhaps Sharaku (active 1794–5), are not represented in the Victoria and Albert Museum's collections.

For a hundred years and more the subject-matter of the print was dominated by actors and courtesans. After an unsteady start, during which first women actors and then, in 1652, young boys were banned from the stage by the authorities, the popular·kabuki theatre developed rapidly, with specially trained adult males taking the female parts. The kabuki is very much a theatre of virtuoso actors and it is the style of acting, rather than the stories, which constitutes its single most distinctive feature. The actors could, if they were successful, become extremely rich; their life-styles excited the admiration of the populace and, on occasion, the wrath of the authorities, who attempted to restrain high living by sumptuary edicts and other restrictions. Given the glamorous position which the actors held (comparable with that of film-stars in the Hollywood era), it was natural that they should be an important source of subject-matter for print designers.

For fifty years the actor print was the special domain of the Torii family of designers, prints by two of whom, Kiyonobu and Kiyomitsu, are reproduced here (PLATES 3 and 4). Kiyonobu was born in Osaka, the son of a man who painted signboards for kabuki theatres, but in 1687 the family moved to Edo and the influence of Moronobu is evident in many of Kiyonobu's prints. On his father's death in 1702 Kiyonobu became head of the school; in fact, he is usually regarded as the founding father of the actor print. In the present example, which can be dated to around 1725 on the basis of theatrical records (the actors themselves being identified by the signs on their costumes), Kiyonobu has left behind the influence of Moronobu and has established a monumental, iconic style, with more attention given to the fall of draperies and the pose than to individual facial expression. This style was to dominate the actor print for much of the next forty years, as we can see from the print of about 1760 by Kiyomitsu, the third master of the Torii line.

Katsukawa Terushige, an obscure artist who was probably a pupil of Kiyonobu, was the designer of our first print (PLATE 5) depicting a scene in the Yoshiwara, the pleasure quarter of Edo, a world unto itself where class barriers between merchants, samurai (who were legally barred but entered regularly under the thinnest of disguises) and actors lost their meaning. Although the best quality girls were extremely expensive, money was by no means everything in the Yoshiwara and the higher class courtesans could spurn with impunity the advances of a rich but boorish client. As well as providing the services which would be expected of them all over the world, the courtesans were often accomplished musicians, versifiers and conversationalists and the best of them might in time be able to save enough money to buy themselves out or even to marry a rich admirer. The print shows a girl and her lover warming themselves at a kotatsu, a kind of covered stove. The youth, whose sword lies in the background, holds a pipe in one hand and in the other a note,

Abbildung 3

Torii Kiyonobu (1664–1729)
Der Schauspieler Sodezaki Iseno, ein
Mädchen darstellend, wird vom
Schauspieler Ogino Isaburō
umarmt, der einen *Samurai* spielt.
Handkoloriert und mit Messing-
staub verziert.
Verlagsmarke und Siegel
Signiert *Torii Kiyonobu hitsu*
Um 1726
31,75×15,2 cm
E. 53–1895

Abbildung 4

Torii Kiyomitsu (1735–1785)
Der Schauspieler *Sakata Hangorō I*
als *Yamada Saburō.*
Mit einem Gedicht.
Verlagsmarken und Siegel
Signiert *Torii Kiyomitsu ga*
Um 1760
31,4×14,6 cm
E. 289–1952 Vermächtnis Shipman

**PLATE 5**

Katsukawa Terushige (active *c.* 1715–*c.* 1725). Couple warming
themselves by a *kotatsu*. Handcoloured. A poem has been added in
manuscript. Publisher's jar-shaped mark. The painting in the alcove
signed *Katsukawa Teru*. Signed on the screen *Katsukawa Terushige*.
20.3 × 29.2 cms (8 × 11.5")
E.609–1899

ses Viertel bildete eine eigene Welt, wo die Klassenschranken zwischen Kaufleuten, Künstlern und *Samurai,* die von Gesetzes wegen nicht zugelassen waren, aber regelmässig unter fadenscheinigem Vorwand Einlass begehrten, ihre Bedeutung verloren. Obwohl die besten Mädchen ausserordentlich teuer waren, war Geld im Yoshiwara keineswegs ausschlaggebend, und die Kurtisanen höherer Klasse konnten ungestraft die Annäherungsversuche eines reichen, aber ungeschliffenen Kunden ablehnen. Neben der Erfüllung der von ihnen wohl in der ganzen Welt erwarteten Dienste waren die Kurtisanen oft vorzügliche Musikerinnen, Poetinnen und gewandte Gesellschafterinnen, und die besten von ihnen mochten mit der Zeit genug Geld verdient haben, um sich loskaufen oder sogar einen reichen Bewunderer heiraten zu können. Der Holzschnitt zeigt ein Mädchen, das sich mit seinem Liebhaber an einem *Kotatsu,* einer Art zugedecktem Ofen, wärmt. Der junge Mann, dessen Schwert im Hintergrund liegt, hält in der einen Hand eine Pfeife und in der anderen einen Zettel, wahrscheinlich einen Liebesbrief. Der Kontrast zwischen dem fliessenden Faltenwurf des Vordergrundes und der eckigen Architektur des Hintergrundes ist typisch für die Interieurs des 18. Jahrhunderts. Einer der Besitzer dieses Holzschnittes muss sich gedacht haben, dass der Liebhaber im Begriffe ist, Abschied zu nehmen, denn das chinesische Gedicht, das irgendwann von einer nicht allzu geübten Hand geschrieben wurde, enthält den Vers: «Ich muss zurückkehren von den grünen Häusern…». Die Bordelle wurden wegen ihrer typischen Fassadenfarbe so genannt.

Der ausgezeichnet erhaltene Holzschnitt von Abbildung 6 ist ein vollendetes Beispiel für die leichte Welt Okumura Toshinobus. Eine auf einem Pferd sitzende Gestalt, die wegen der übertrieben langen Griffe der zwei Schwerter als *Samurai* identifiziert werden kann, wird durch eine Frau des Yoshiwara verführt. Der *Samurai* weist in mildem Protest nach links, aber er ist dem Mädchen keineswegs gewachsen, dessen Name *Nowaki,* Herbststurm, bestimmte Leidenschaften vermuten lässt.

Suzuki Harunobu (Abb. 7) ist der Künstler, der die Zeit des Mehrfarbendruckes einleitete und ihn einem breiteren Publikum zugänglich machte, was jedoch keineswegs seinen einzigen Beitrag zur japanischen Holzschnittkunst darstellt. Er schuf eine neue Welt sanfter Stimmungen, die vor allem durch seine verfeinerten Farbzusammenstellungen und den süssen Ausdruck der nymphenhaften Mädchen, die seine Holzschnitte bevölkern, vermittelt wird; bei diesen Mädchen handelt es sich oft nicht um Bewohnerinnen des Yoshiwara, sondern einfach um Mädchen aus Edo, die ihren alltäglichen Beschäftigungen nachgehen. Abbildung 7 zeigt ein Blatt aus einer seiner berühmten Serien; der im Titel vorkommende Ausdruck «acht Ansichten…» bezog sich ursprünglich auf eine Landschaft in China, doch er wurde von den Holzschnittmeistern als Vorwand für eine Reihe von Darstellungen des Alltagslebens benutzt, was typisch ist für die spielerische Haltung, die sie gegenüber der klassischen Tradition einnehmen. Es ist interessant festzustellen, wie verschieden und doch wirkungsvoll die Farben sind, wenn sie mit der um ein oder zwei Jahre früher, 1766, publizierten Originalausgabe verglichen werden; die von Druck zu Druck variierende Farbgebung ist ein Charakteristikum manch berühmter Holzschnitte, aber wir werden wahrscheinlich nie wissen, ob sie den Wünschen des Künstlers oder eher dem Experimentieren des Druckers zuzuschreiben ist.

Isoda Koryūsai, ein weiterer Künstler aus der frühen Periode des Mehrfarbendruckes, wird durch zwei Holzschnitte vorgestellt, die in seinem be-
vorzugten langen und schmalen Format, *Hashira-e,* gehalten sind, wobei er
erfolgreich die Schwierigkeiten dieses Formates ausnutzte. In der bezau-
bernden Studie eines Mädchens, das seinen Hund neckt, gebraucht er ge-
schickt den langen Griff des Musikinstrumentes, um eine starke und doch
unaufdringliche Diagonale zu schaffen, die die weit voneinander entfern-
ten Elemente der Komposition zusammenhält (Abb.8).

Torii Kiyonaga (Abb.9) war ein Schüler Kiyomitsus, aber seine Theater-
darstellungen bilden keinen wichtigen Teil seiner Arbeit. Seine Spezialität
waren grosse, majestätische Schönheiten, die er gerne im Freien gruppierte,
wo ein sorgfältig gestalteter Hintergrund die Bedeutung der farbenfrohen
und würdigen Darstellungen der Kurtisanen, die träge ihren alltäglichen Beschäftigungen nachgehen, erhöhte. Der Kurtisanen-Holzschnitt wurde um
1780 von seinen Arbeiten beherrscht, und einige Elemente seines Stils hiel-
ten sich noch lange bis ins 19.Jahrhundert hinein, obwohl Kiyonaga das
Entwerfen von Druckvorlagen um 1790 aufgegeben zu haben scheint.

Weiter oben wurden *Shunga,* Erotika, als hier vernachlässigter aber wich-
tiger Arbeitsbereich vieler Künstler erwähnt; dies gilt zum Beispiel für
Kiyonaga trotz der kühlen Eleganz seiner Frauengestalten in seinen übli-
chen Arbeiten. Hauptsächlich wegen der oft in grotesker Weise über-
triebenen Grösse der Geschlechtsorgane scheinen uns viele *Shunga* lächer-
lich; Shunchōs Darstellung jedoch (Abb.10) weist diese Schwäche weniger
auf. Für den modernen Betrachter wenigstens handelt es sich fraglos nicht
um eine pornographische, sondern um eine feinfühlige Darstellung.

Utamaro (Abb.11) beherrschte die Zeit um 1790 ähnlich wie Kiyonaga das
vorangegangene Jahrzehnt. Er ist einer der grössten Holzschnittkünstler der
Welt und verzeichnete viele Erfolge, wobei er vielleicht heute vor allem
wegen der Ausdruckskraft, die seinen Darstellungen weiblicher Schönheit
eigen sind, bewundert wird. Weder konnte Harunobu mit seinem liebens-
würdigen Charme, noch Kiyonaga mit seiner würdigen Vornehmheit die
Figuren mit soviel individuellem Charme beseelen wie Utamaro, der unter
die Oberfläche drang, um Schönheiten zu erschaffen, deren differenzierte
Persönlichkeiten dem Betrachter mit der äussersten Sparsamkeit und Zart-
heit vermittelt werden.

Utamaros Einfluss war gross, und viele seiner Zeitgenossen entwarfen
Holzschnitte, die einen Vergleich mit seinen eigenen Meisterwerken be-
stehen können. Drei Beispiele, die alle um die Mitte des grossen Jahrzehnts
Utamaros datieren, werden hier wiedergegeben. Abbildung 12 zeigt einen
berühmten Entwurf Chōbunsai Eishis, dessen besondere Stellung unter den
grossen *Ukiyo-e*-Künstlern darin besteht, dass er der Sohn eines hohen Re-
gierungsbeamten war, dass er also eher von der *Samurai*-Klasse abstammte
als vom gewöhnlichen Volk. Die betont in die Länge gezogene Gestalt, übri-
gens auch ein Zug vieler Holzschnitte Utamaros desselben Datums, und der
eher hochmütige Ausdruck ermutigen nicht, sich für Itsutomis menschliche
Qualitäten zu erwärmen. Eishi ist ein weniger guter Beobachter der mensch-
lichen Natur als sein grosser Zeitgenosse, doch die hervorragende dekora-
tive Wirkung, die hier durch einen Glimmergrund gesteigert wird, und die
ausgezeichnete Komposition bedeuten mehr als nur eine Kompensation für
das Fehlen jedes psychologischen Scharfblicks. Wir befinden uns in der gol-
denen Zeit der *Ōkubi-e,* der Brustbilder, und obwohl Utamaro auf diesem

PLATE 7
Suzuki Harunobu (died 1770)
Returning sails of the towel rack,
from the series *Zashiki Hakkei*,
eight views of the parlour
*c.* 1768
26.4 × 20.6 cms (10.4 × 8.1″)
E.55–1955

PLATE 8a
Isoda Koryūsai
(active *c.* 1764–1780s)
Girl teasing her dog with a *samisen*
*Hashirae* (pillar-print)
Signed *Koryūsai ga* with a seal
*Masakatsu*
*c.* 1775
69.5 × 12.1 cms (27.4 × 4.75″)
E.3756–1953   Horn Bequest

PLATE 8b
Isoda Koryūsai
A courtesan's lucky dream
*Hashirae* (pillar-print)
Signed *Koryū ga*
69.5 × 12.1 (27.4 × 4.75″)
E.3757–1953   Horn Bequest

Abbildung 9

Torii Kiyonaga (1752–1815)
Ein Spaziergang in den Vorstädten.
Verlagsmarken
Jedes Blatt signiert *Kiyonaga ga*
Um 1780
38,7×76,2 cm
E. 392–1895

Abbildung 10

Katsukawa Shunchō (aktiv etwa 1780–1795)
Liebespaar auf einem Balkon, aus der Serie *Kōshoku zue junikō*, die zwölf Stunden der Liebe, illustriert.
Um 1790
24,8×37,4 cm
E. 225–1968

21

*ōkubie* and the statuesque full-length courtesans typified by Eishi's print) and he was especially fond of giving his figures an atmospheric background such as a night sky filled with fireflies, a fall of snow or, as here, a gently rippling sea contrasting sharply with a mica-decorated sky and a strongly coloured sun. The setting of the figure against the background is the key to the marvellous compositional unity of this design, a unity which is underlined by the choice of colour for background and foreground. This is a print of which many varying states exist, with marked differences in background detail and even in the mood suggested by the girl's face. In the copy illustrated the unity of the girl and her setting seems to be enhanced by her expression, which conveys a sense of refined expectation entirely appropriate to the first day of the year.

By 1760, the approximate date of Kiyomitsu's print (PLATE 4), the actor portrait seemed to have entered a stylistic groove from which it might never emerge, but ten years later, in 1770, the transformation of this particular area of *ukiyoe* art was heralded by the publication of *Ehon Butai no Ōgi*, a picture book of fans for the stage, designed by Ippitsusai Bunchō and Katsukawa Shunshō, which consists of three volumes of bust portraits of actors on fan-shaped backgrounds. Unlike most previous actor prints the portraits by these two artists were individually characterised; from then on it would no longer be necessary to identify actors by the crests on their costumes or by inscriptions giving their names. In his actor prints Shunshō stresses too the dramatic qualities inherent in each theatrical situation: in the triptych reproduced here (PLATE 15), it seems clear enough that the two flanking figures are rivals for the affections of the central courtesan and each face expresses the appropriate emotion as well as being recognisable as that of a known individual actor. It is noteworthy that Shunshō did not limit himself to depicting actors on the stage; in his pursuit of the individual character of each star he went behind the scenes for some perceptive studies of actors preparing in their dressing rooms or relaxing at home.

A favourite role of the Ichikawa Danjūrō line of actors was the interlude known as *Shibaraku*, 'wait a moment!'. This interlude, in which a fearless *samurai* rescues a young couple from execution, was invented in 1697 by the first Danjūrō and performed by members of the Ichikawa family on countless occasions from then on. Few actor-print artists could resist the temptation of the design possibilities offered by the striking striped make-up, the great badges of the Ichikawa family and the comically huge sword. Utagawa Toyokuni (PLATE 16) alone is known to have produced several prints of the subject. The print shows Ichikawa Danjūrō VII, perhaps the supreme theatrical giant of the nineteenth century, in his debut

PLATE 11
Kitagawa Utamaro (1754–1806)
*Yoso iku no kihan*, boats returning from a visit to another place, from the series *Fūzoku ukiyo hakkei*, up-to-date eight views of the floating world
Publisher's mark
Signed *Utamaro hitsu*
Early 1790s
38.1 × 25.1 cms (15 × 9.9″)
E.3244–1953   Lee Bequest

23

24

△ PLATE 13  Hosoda Eishō (active *c.* 1780– *c.* 1800). The courtesan *Yosooi* of the
*Matsubaya.* Publisher's mark. Signed *Shōeidō Eishō ga.* 1790s
38.4 × 25.4 cms (15.1 × 10″). E.1414–1898

◁ PLATE 12  Chōbunsai Eishi (1756–1829). The courtesan *Itsutomi* holding the
plectrum for a samisen which lies behind her, from the series *Seirō geisha sen*,
selected entertainers of the green houses. Publisher's mark, censor's seal
Signed *Eishi zu. c.* 1795. 39.4 × 26 cms (15.5 × 10.2″). E.3762–1953
Horn Bequest

as a fully-fledged actor; to honour the occasion a congratulatory poem is inscribed above.

Most of the prints discussed here are by artists who lived in Edo, but it seems only just that the great Osaka tradition of theatrical print design should be represented by one example (PLATE 17) which illustrates well the distinctive style of the great commercial centre of western Japan. The abiding influence of Shunshō can be seen in the individuality and drama of the face – a feature which Hokushū in fact intensified in this striking portrait of another great actor, Nakamura Utaemon III. The use of the fan to concentrate attention on the facial expression is a favourite Osaka device; and mirrors and circular reserves were frequently used in the same way.

The demand for actor prints and pictures of courtesans continued throughout the nineteenth century, but although many splendid designs were produced in response to this demand they are not the most characteristic products of the age and it is not by them that the later period of *ukiyoe* is best known. From about 1820 onwards the most important and most innovative prints are the landscapes, the warrior prints and, to a lesser extent, the bird and flower studies and the still-lifes. When, in the 1850s and 1860s, European contact with Japan was resumed, the first *ukiyoe* prints to reach artists in Paris and London were those which were currently for sale on the streets of Edo and Yokohama so that even today Hokusai, Hiroshige and Kuniyoshi, the great nineteenth century trio, are better known to most westerners than the masters of the eighteenth century, with the possible exception of Utamaro. The two Japanese prints most famous in the West are probably the *Great Wave off Kanagawa* and the *Fuji in Clear Weather* (PLATE 18) both by Hokusai. But as we marvel at the majestic simplicity of the design we would do well to remember that Hokusai had been artistically active for more than forty years when it was published; he had done actor prints in the style of Shunshō and beauties under the influence of Kiyonaga; he had established the *surimono* greeting cards (see below) as an important minor art form and he had produced countless sketches and illustrated books. Many of these aspects of his work are only a little better appreciated today than they were at the end of the nineteenth century.

If Hokusai's landscapes are celebrated above all for the almost abstract grandeur and simplicity of their design, for the skill with which all inessentials are cut away in the interests of total effect, we admire his great contemporary and successor Hiroshige for sensitive depiction of the everchanging moods of nature and sympathetic portrayal of man in his physical environment. Hiroshige is the great master of rain, whether it be the squally showers in his famous

PLATE 14
Eishōsai Chōki
(active *c.* 1786–*c.* 1805)
Sunrise on New Year's Day
Publisher's mark, censor's seal
Signed *Chōki ga*
1790s
38.7 × 24.8 cms (15.25 × 9.75")
E.3774–1953   Horn Bequest

△ PLATE 15
Katsukawa Shunshō (1726–1792). Scene from a play
Left to right: Ichikawa Danjūrō V, Segawa Kikunojō, Ichimura
Uzaemon. Signed on each sheet, *Shunshō ga. c.* 1780.
30.5 × 42.9 cms (12 × 16.9″). E.1282–1896

▷ PLATE 16
Utagawa Toyokuni (1769–1825). The actor *Ichikawa Danjūrō* VII in
a *shibaraku* role. Inscribed with a poem. Publisher's mark, censor's seal
Signed *Toyokuni ga.* 1807. 38.7 × 27.3 cms (15.25 × 10.75″)
E.12646–1886

print of *Shōno*, with travellers rushing for shelter, or the long
drenching downpour of *Night Rain at Karasaki* from the *Eight Views
of Lake Biwa*. He captured the atmosphere of this latter print again in
a fan print (PLATE 19), *Night Rain at Eitai Bridge*, where the atmosphere of overpowering stillness broken only by the sound of rain
falling is emphasised – a typical Hiroshige touch – by the presence
of bowed figures in straw hats and raincoats poling their vessels.
Hiroshige is best known, perhaps, for his two great landscape and
travel series, *The Fifty-three Stations on the Tōkaidō Road* and the
*Sixty-nine Stations on the Kisokaidō Road* (the latter set done in collaboration with a lesser artist, Keisai Eisen). To represent these another
weather dominated scene has been chosen (PLATE 20); as in
Hiroshige's studies of rain the skill and patience of the block-cutters
contributes much to the effect, but it is the treatment of the human
figures which lends the print its special atmosphere.

This brief selection of landscapes concludes with Yashima Gakutei,
a lesser-known artist, whose work shows the influence of Hokusai,
sometimes in direct adaptation of the master's designs, sometimes
merely in the quasi-geometric simplicity of approach. In the 1830s
Gakutei lived in Osaka, whose local scenery inspired him to produce
his best-known series, the views of Mount Tempō. The brilliantly
effective colour scheme and quiet grandeur of PLATE 21 place it
almost on a level with some of Hokusai's greatest designs.

It was explained above that the commissioning of calendar prints
for private circulation encouraged the development of full-colour
printing in *ukiyoe* style; in fact these calendars have a double impor-
tance, for there also developed from them a tradition of privately
printed greeting cards of all kinds which formed a significant part
of print production during the late eighteenth and early nineteenth
centuries. These special prints, called *surimono* (meaning no more
than 'rubbed [i.e. printed Japanese-style] thing') were published in
small numbers and not sold on the open market. They were com-
missioned by wealthy men and were usually sent on special occasions. For all these reasons a great deal of care and attention was
lavished on their production, with extreme precision in the printing,
great subtlety of colouring and liberal use of such techniques as
blind-printing and decoration with metal dusts. That indefatigable
innovator Hokusai was largely responsible, it seems, for the spread
in popularity of these exquisitely-printed items but we reproduce
here a print by a lesser-known artist, Kubo Shumman (PLATE 22)
who made something of a speciality of them. Typical features include bold use of blind printing and poems, presumably by members
of the charmingly named 'Mist Club' which appears to have com-
missioned the series.

PLATE 18 Katsushika Hokusai (1760–1849). *Gaifū kaisei*, a gentle breeze and clear weather, from *Fugaku sanjūrokkei*, thirty-six views of Mount Fuji. Signed *Hokusai aratame Iitsu hitsu* Late 1820s. 24.8 × 36.2 cms (9.75 × 14.25″). E.4813–1916. Alexander Gift

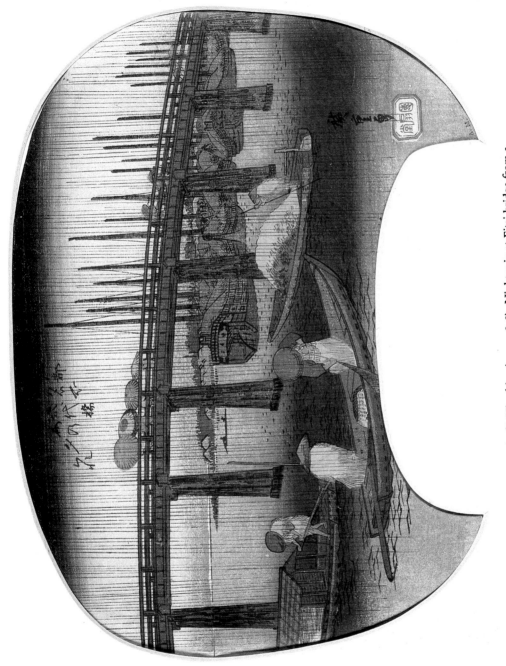

PLATE 19  Andō Hiroshige (1797–1858).  Night rain at Eitai bridge from a
series *Kōto meisho*, views of Edo (Tokyo). Publisher's seal. Signed *Hiroshige ga*
*c.* 1840.  22.2 × 29.5 cms (8.75 × 11.6″).  E.4938–1919

PLATE 20  Andō Hiroshige (1797–1858) *Ōi*, number 47 from the series *Kisokaidō rokujūkyū tsugi no uchi*, from the 69 stations on the Kisokaidō road. Publisher's and censor's seals. Signed *Hiroshige ga* with a seal *Ichiryūsai. c.* 1840. 26 × 36.8 cms (10.25 × 14.5″). E.3802–1886

**PLATE 21** Yashima Gakutei (c. 1786–1868). *Tempōzan mansen nyūshin no zu*, fleet of ships entering Tempōzan harbour from the series *Tempōzan shōkei ichiran*, views of Mt Tempō. Signed *Gogaku* with a mark. 1830s. 25.2 × 36.8 cms (10 × 14.5″). E.745–1910

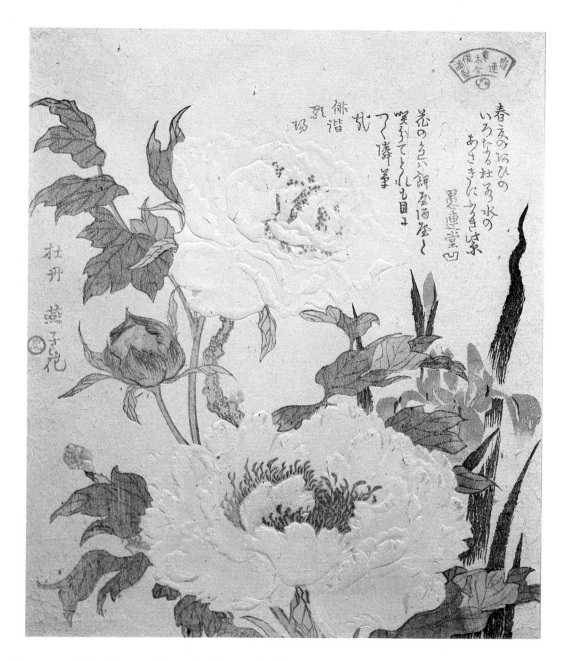

△ PLATE 22  Kubo Shumman (1757–1820). *Botan* and *enshika*, peonies
and irises. Inscribed with poems. With a fan-shaped seal: *Karen kusaki awase
Shumman sei*, a collection of plants done for the Mist Club by Shumman.
20.6 × 18.1 cms (8.1 × 7.1″). E.12–1895

▷ PLATE 23  Katsushika Hokusai (1760–1849). *Kawasemi, ayame* and *nadeshiko*,
kingfisher, irises and pinks, from the series often called the 'Small Flowers'
Inscribed with a poem. Publisher's mark, censor's seal. Signed *Zen Hokusai
Iitsu hitsu. c.* 1830. 22.9 × 16.5 cms (9 × 6.5″). E.599–1899

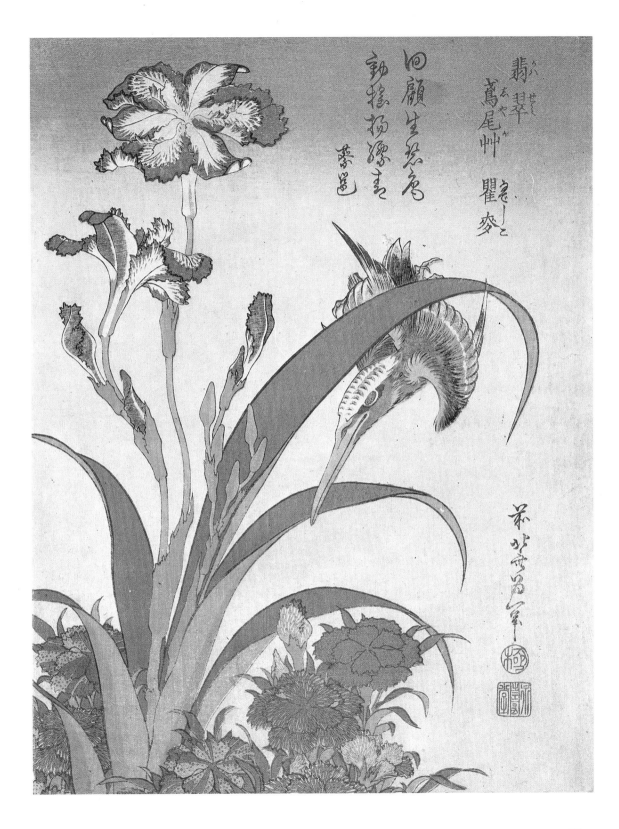

37

Even if we confine our attention to his prints and ignore his illustrated books, drawings and paintings, the artistic output of Hokusai during the years 1825–1833 is truly amazing. In addition to the *Thirty-Six Views of Mount Fuji* (in fact there are 46 in all), he published sets of ghost stories, famous bridges, waterfalls and Chinese and Japanese poets as well as two floral series, one with flowers alone and the other with birds added (PLATE 23). In fact almost all of his work which is well-known in the West was produced in this short period of less than a decade. Hokusai was always seeking to broaden the horizons of his art and although both landscapes and bird-and-flower prints (*kachōe*) had been designed by earlier *ukiyoe* artists it was he who elevated both of them to the status of major areas of subject matter, on a par with courtesans and actors.

The search for new themes during the nineteenth century led to the rise of the warrior print, whose greatest master was Utagawa Kuniyoshi (PLATES 24 and 25). He was another fascinatingly many-sided individual, who studied a huge range of artists and styles (including, like Hokusai, European painting which he discovered through prints brought to Japan by Dutch traders) and tried his hand at every conceivable type of subject. But in spite of his landscapes and his Chinese legends, with their European-looking perspective and shading, he continues to be admired most of all for his warrior prints. As his celebrated heroic triptychs lose so much when reduced in size, we have chosen for reproduction a single sheet print (PLATE 24) from a series produced during one of his most fertile periods. Kuniyoshi's skill in depicting violent and sanguinary conflict is self-evident. His interest in the past was, however, by no means confined to warfare and around 1840 he published a fine series of prints of some of the 'Hundred Poets' (PLATE 25). These poets were the authors of a hundred poems selected in 1235 by the famous Fujiwara no Sadaie (often called Teika) and it is clear that in designing the series Kuniyoshi was conscious of the classical nature of the subject. Especially in his depiction of figures in court dress and his choice of colours, his debt to the narrative scrolls of the mediaeval period is very evident.

Kuniyoshi had many pupils, some of whom produced work of feeble quality and quite staggering dullness but in Yoshitoshi (PLATE 26) he had a worthy successor. As this posthumously published print shows, the printers of the Meiji period (1868–1912) reached new heights of technical expertise: the water which surrounds the two combatants is suggested by streaks of chemical blue whose delicate shading must have required very painstaking blockcutting and careful wiping of the ink before printing. The ferocious expressions and the elaborately detailed blockcarving represent the ultimate development of the style inaugurated by Kuniyoshi.

PLATE 24
Utagawa Kuniyoshi (1797–1861)
The warrior-monk *Negoro no Komizucha* amid a hail of weapons, number 26 from the series *Taiheiki Eiyūden*, stories of outstanding bravery in the 16th century wars
Narrative text by *Ryūkatei Tanekazu* (1807–1858)
Publisher's mark, censors' seals
Signed *Ichiyūsai Kuniyoshi ga*
1847–1850
35.3 × 25 cms (13.9 × 9.8″)
E.10799–1886

40

PLATE 25
Utagawa Kuniyoshi (1797–1861)
*Arihara no Narihira Ason* watching
maple leaves floating down the
Tatsuta river, number 17 from the
series *Hyakunin isshu no uchi*, a
hundred poems by a hundred
poets
Publisher's mark
Signed *Chōōrō Kuniyoshi ga* with
seal-mark
*c.* 1840–1842
35.9 × 24.1 cms (14.1 × 9.5″)
E.11411–1886

PLATE 26
Tsukioka Yoshitoshi (1839–1892)
*Rōrihakuchō Chōjun* and *Kokusempū
Riki* fighting underwater, a scene
from the novel *Suikoden*, a
translation of the Chinese novel
*Shui hu chuan,* 'The Water
Margin'
Publisher's inscription
Signed *Kaisai Yoshitoshi ga* with a
seal *Taiso*
1900
71.1 × 24.4 cms (28 × 9.6″)
E.1028–1914   Noguchi Gift

41

PLATE 27  Yamada Kuniteru (1829–1874) *Tōkyō Nihombashi no kei*, a view of
Nihon bridge, Tokyo. Publisher's marks, censor's seals. Signed *Ichiyōsai Kuniteru ga* and
*motome ni ōjite*, by special request, *Kuniteru ga*. 1870. 36.3 × 70.4 cms (14.3 × 27.7")
E.99–1969   Shelving Bequest

PLATE 28   ? Tsukioka Kōgyo (1869–1927). A squadron of our destroyers engages in close and bitter fighting with an enemy battleship outside Port Arthur and inflicts a major defeat on April 13th 1904. Publisher's inscription
Signed ? Kōkyo and *motome ni ōjite*, by special request, with an undeciphered seal
Published April 20th 1904. 38.1 × 76.2 cms (15 × 30"). E.3140–1905

44

In 1854 a treaty was signed between the United States and Japan and two ports were opened to American trade; the other great powers quickly followed suit and soon the wholesale westernisation and modernisation of Japan was in full swing. In 1868 the power of the emperor was restored and the capital was renamed Tokyo. Foreigners appeared on the streets of the great cities and western-style carriages and omnibuses came into use. The opportunities afforded by this novel subject-matter prevented the landscape print from going into total decline, as Kuniteru's interesting scene shows (PLATE 27).

Japanese block-carvers worked fast and actor portraits usually came out within a few days of the first performance of a play. This speed of production was utilised for the last time during the Sino-Japanese (1894–5) and Russo–Japanese (1904–5) wars, when a number of obscure artists, among them Kōkyo or Kōgyo (PLATE 28), were employed to produce stirringly patriotic scenes of military valour and efficiency which were on sale in Tokyo within as little as a week of the action taking place.

Leaping on half a century we come to the work of Munakata Shikō (PLATE 29), the greatest exponent of the modern print movement. All the conventions of the old prints of Edo are cast aside by this pugnacious artist, who was born far from Tokyo in the often-snowbound northernmost part of Honshu, the main island of Japan. After a youthful dalliance with western painting techniques, Munakata decided in the late 1920s that he should return to an essentially Japanese method of self-expression and he rapidly created a new and personal style whose main features are great boldness and, very often, profound religious intensity. His imaginative vitality bodes well for the Japanese print which is at present enjoying a powerful, many-sided and one hopes, long-lived revival.

# Books for Further Reading

The literature of the Japanese print is enormous and only a few of the most essential books in English are mentioned here. The largest selection of prints from the Victoria and Albert Museum's own collections will be found in R. A. Crighton, *The Floating World, Japanese popular prints 1700–1900*, London, 1973, where about three hundred are reproduced with useful captions. A good if somewhat old-fashioned general introduction, which combines thorough scholarship with interesting aesthetic judgements, is Laurence Binyon and J. J. O'Brien Sexton, *Japanese Colour Prints*, London, 1923 and 1960. Richard Lane, *Images from the Floating World*, Oxford, 1978, is a more up-to-date survey, but there is an unnecessarily strong emphasis on *shunga* and some of the opinions expressed are eccentric. The book includes a 150 page *Illustrated Dictionary of* Ukiyo-e, which contains much useful information, some of it drawn from other secondary sources. Other good general works (both of them consisting of full-page illustrations with extensive commentaries) are Narazaki Muneshige, *The Japanese Print: its Evolution and Essence*, Tokyo, 1966 and Harold P. Stern, *Master Prints of Japan*, New York, 1969. The text of the latter book is particularly lively and sensitive. For an example of in-depth cataloguing displaying profound knowledge of the literary, social and theatrical background of each print illustrated, David Waterhouse, *Images of Eighteenth-Century Japan*, Toronto, 1975, is recommended. A superb catalogue of a great collection is Jack Hillier, *Japanese Prints and Drawings from the Vever Collection*, London, 1976, which has nearly a thousand entries. For biographical details of artists the best reference book is L. P. Roberts, *A Dictionary of Japanese Artists*, New York and Tokyo, 1976. The coverage of the print artists is excellent: characters are given for all the different names and where there is factual uncertainty the different scholarly opinions are set out. There is also an extensive bibliography.

Works on individual artists are recommended as follows (in alphabetical order of artist):

Jack Hillier, *Suzuki Harunobu*, Philadelphia, 1970.
D. B. Waterhouse, *Harunobu and his Age*, London, 1964.
B. W. Robinson, *Hiroshige*, London, 1964.
Jack Hillier, *Hokusai*, London, 1955 and 1978.
Chieko Hirano, *Kiyonaga*, Cambridge, Mass., 1939.
B. W. Robinson, *Kuniyoshi*, London, 1961.
Jack Hillier, *Utamaro*, London, 1961 and 1979.

The following specialist works are recommended:

David Chibbett, *The History of Japanese Printing and Book Illustration*, Tokyo, New York and San Francisco, 1977.
M. Ishida, *Japanese Buddhist Prints*, Tokyo, 1964.
M. Kawakita, *Contemporary Japanese Prints*, Tokyo, 1967.
R. S. Keyes and Keiko Mizushima, *The Theatrical World of Osaka Prints*, Philadelphia, 1973.
K. Meissner, *Surimono*, London, n.d. (*c.* 1970).
O. Statler, *Modern Japanese Prints*, Rutland, Vermont and Tokyo, 1956.
T. Yoshida and R. Yuki, *Japanese Print-Making*, Rutland, Vermont and Tokyo, 1966. Deals with contemporary and traditional techniques.

# Index of Artists

*Figures in normal type refer to page numbers, those in italics to plate numbers.*